Standards

Arranged by Dan Coates

CONTENTS

Copyright © MMIX by Alfred Publishing Co., Inc.
All Rights Reserved   Printed in USA

Alfred

ISBN-10: 0-7390-6006-6
ISBN-13: 978-0-7390-6006-3

COME RAIN OR COME SHINE

Lyrics by Johnny Mercer
Music by Harold Arlen
Arranged by Dan Coates

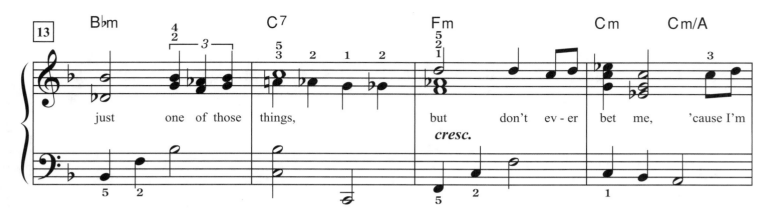

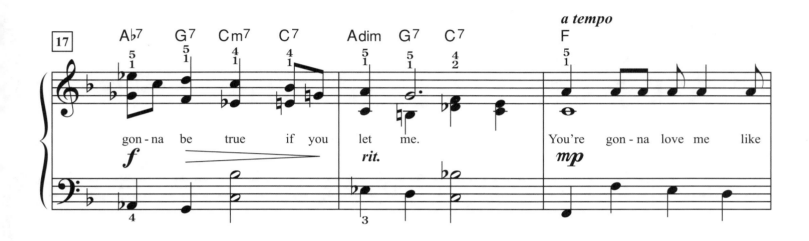

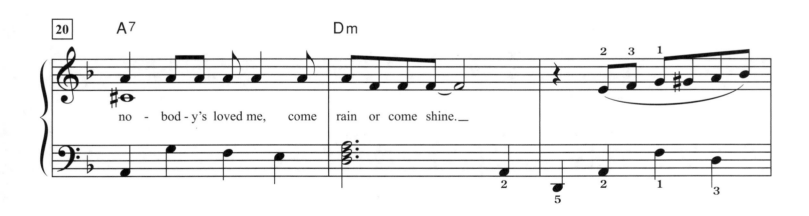

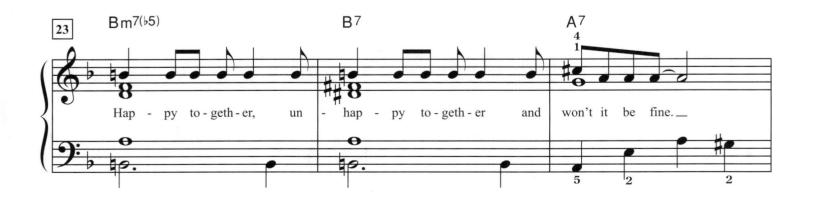

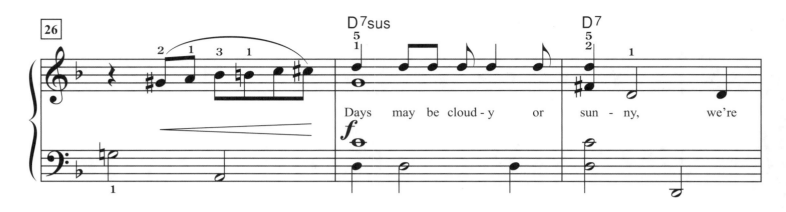

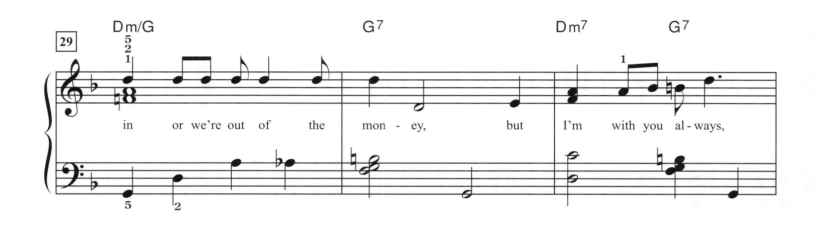

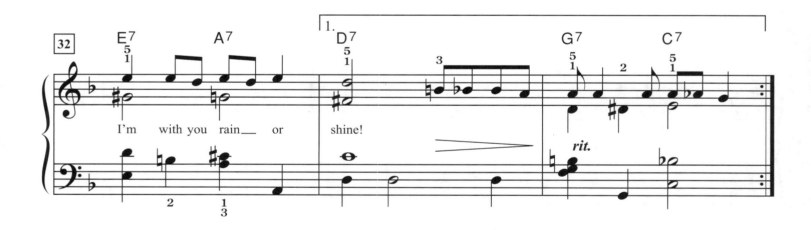

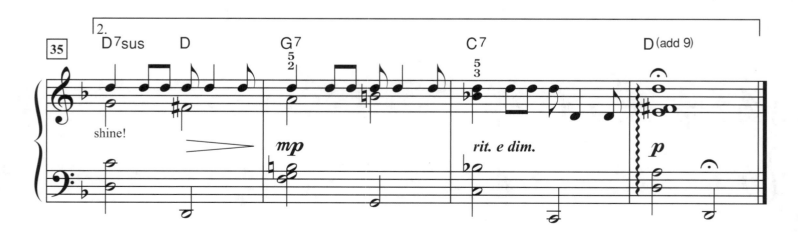

FLY ME TO THE MOON

Words and Music by Bart Howard
Arranged by Dan Coates

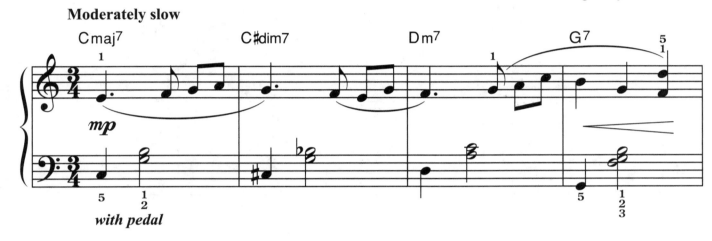

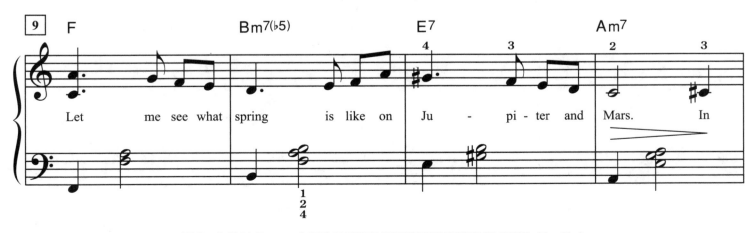

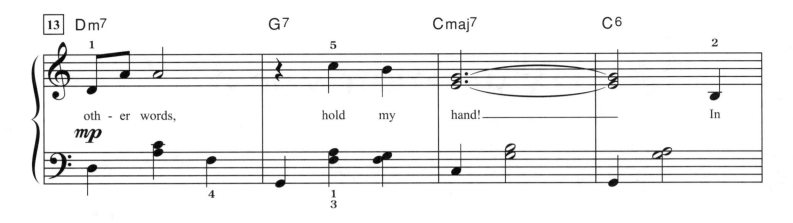

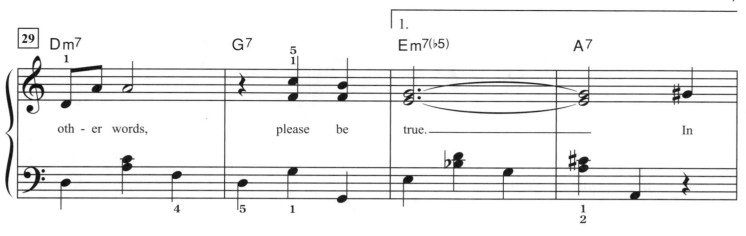

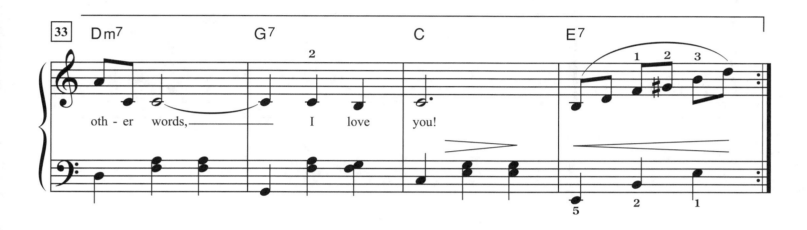

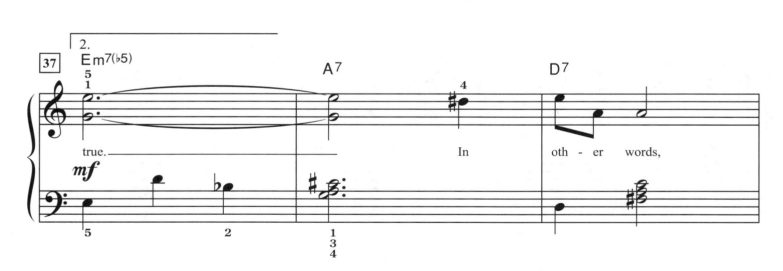

I COULD WRITE A BOOK

Words by Lorenz Hart
Music by Richard Rodgers
Arranged by Dan Coates

Slowly, with expression

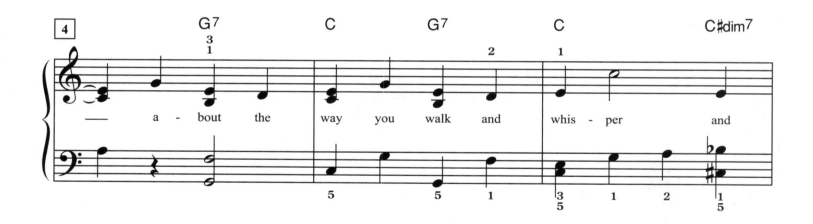

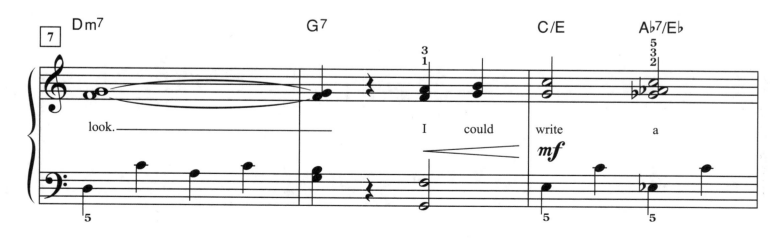

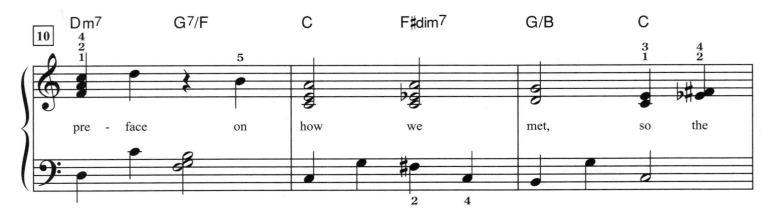

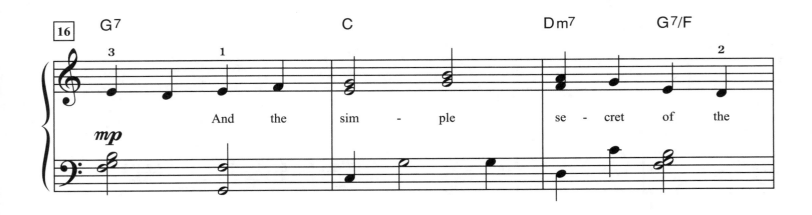

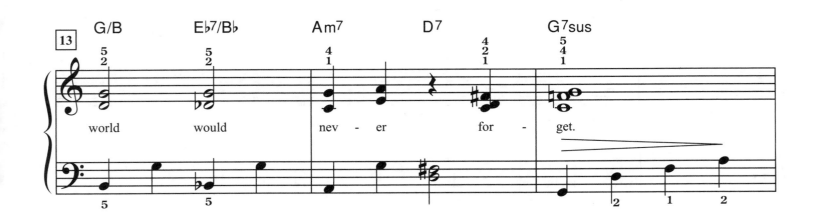

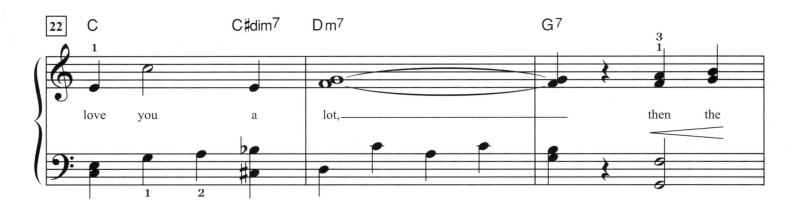

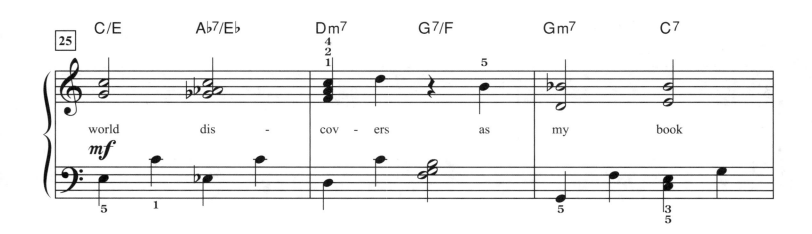

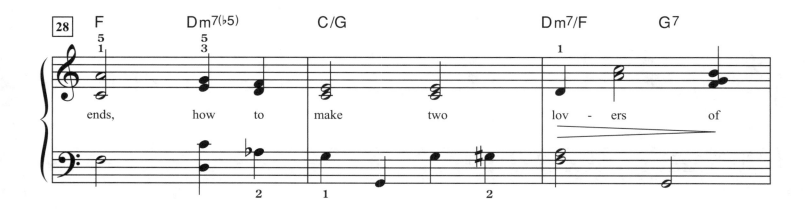

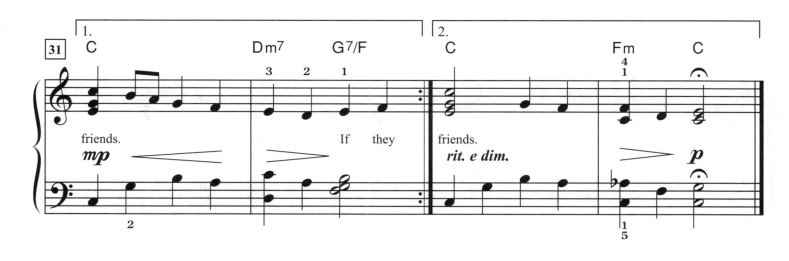

I GET A KICK OUT OF YOU

Words and Music by Cole Porter
Arranged by Dan Coates

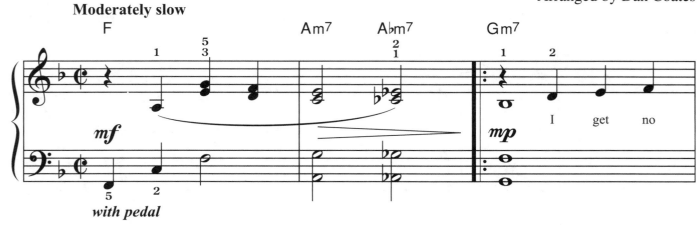

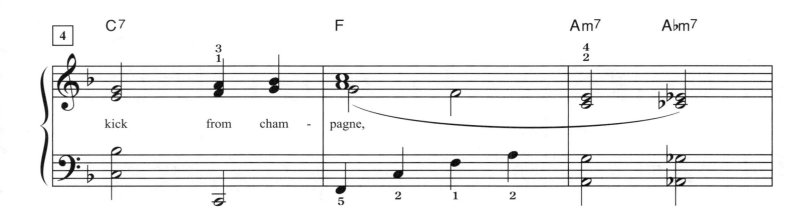

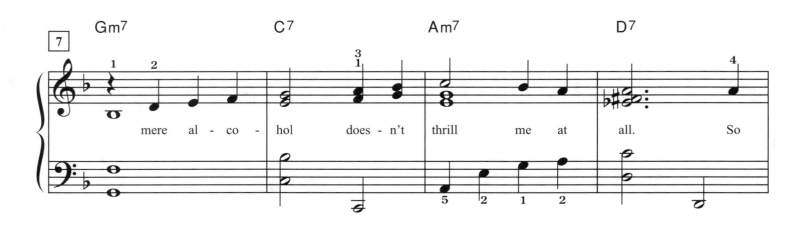

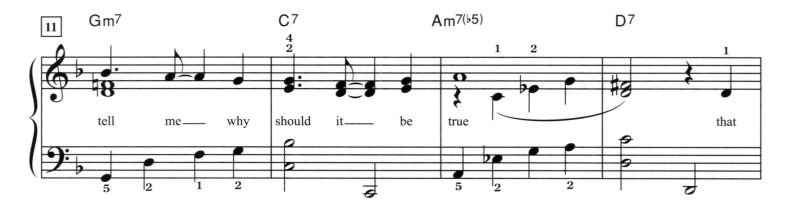

tell me—— why should it—— be true that

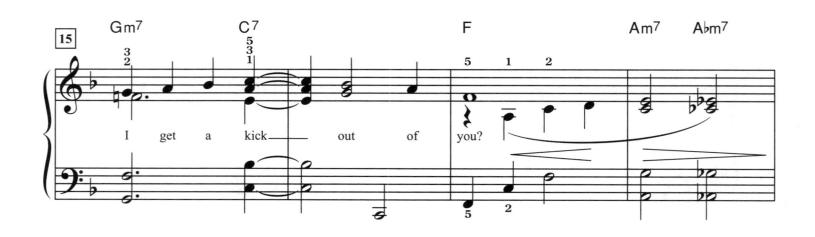

I get a kick—— out of you?

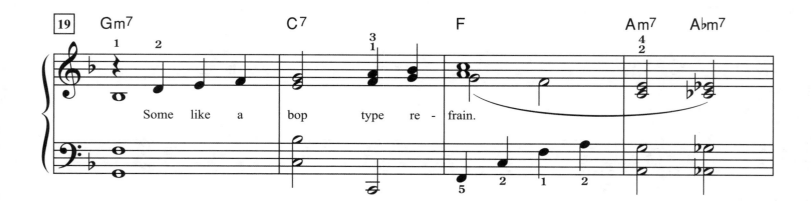

Some like a bop type re - frain.

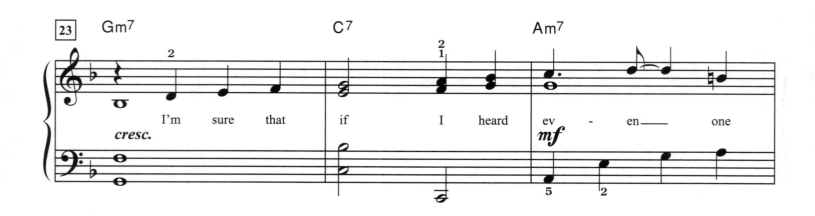

I'm sure that if I heard ev - en—— one

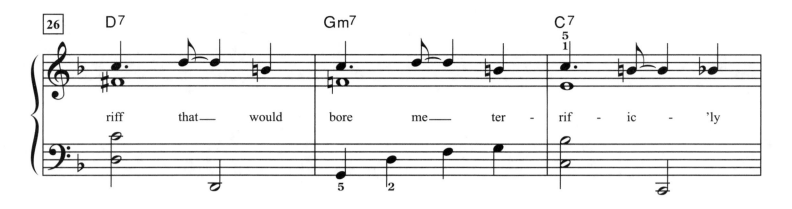

riff that— would bore me— ter - rif - ic - 'ly

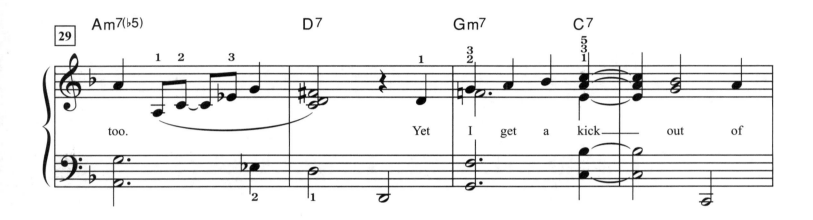

too. Yet I get a kick— out of

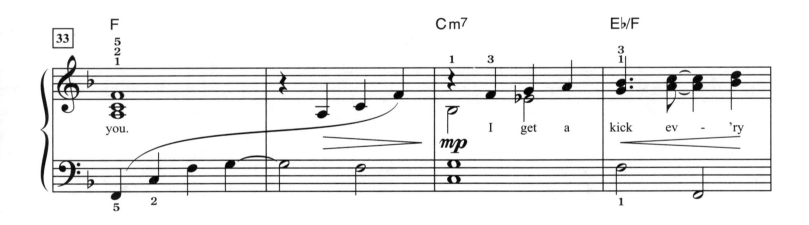

you. I get a kick ev - 'ry

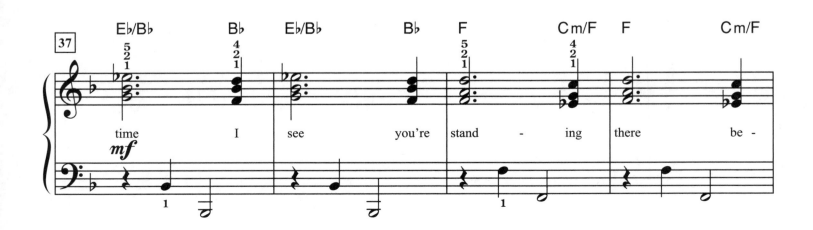

time I see you're stand - ing there be -

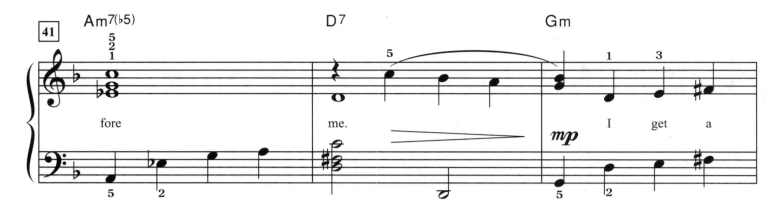

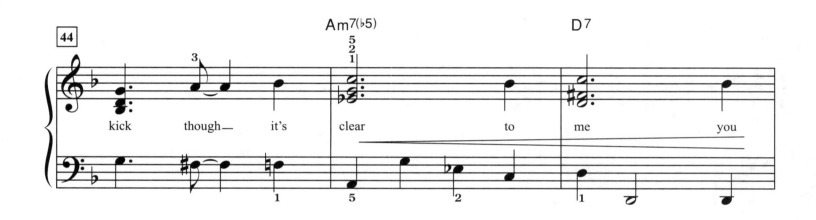

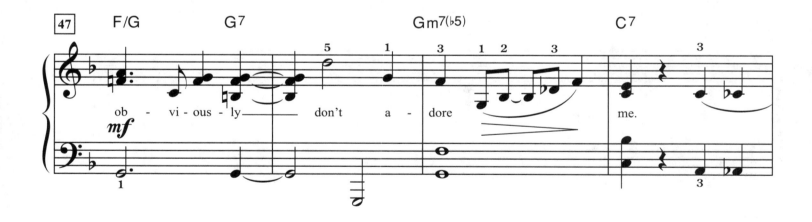

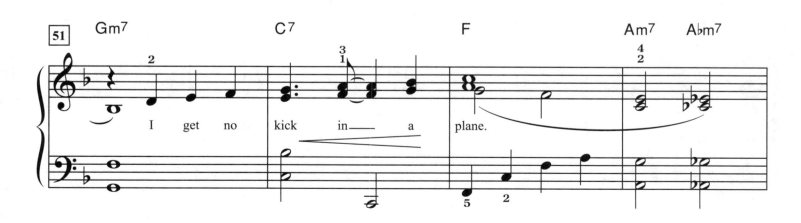

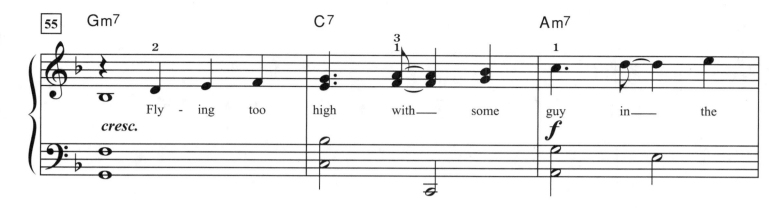

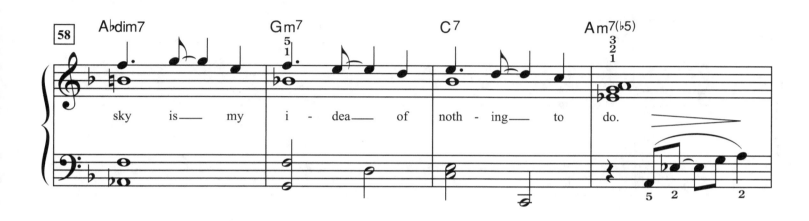

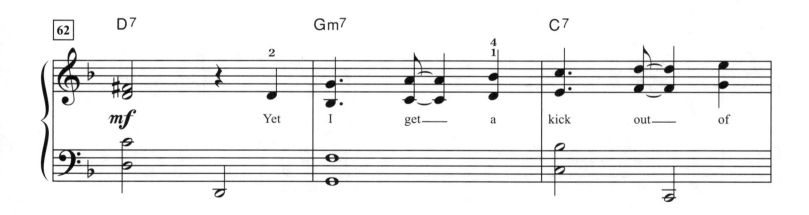

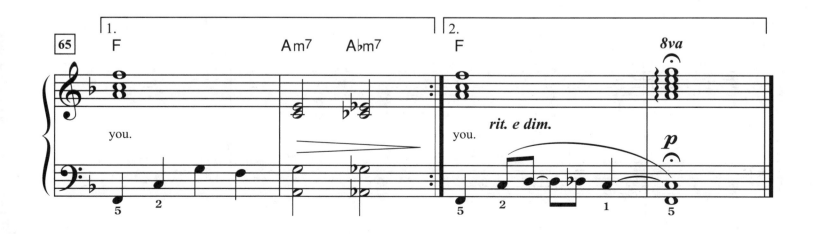

I'VE GOT YOU UNDER MY SKIN

Words and Music by Cole Porter
Arranged by Dan Coates

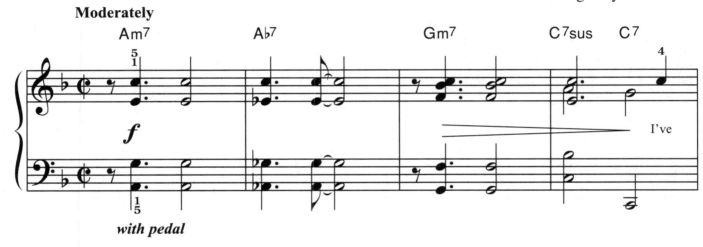

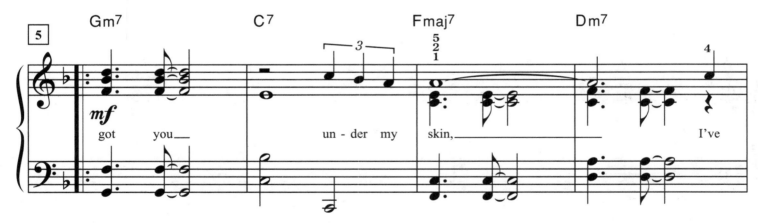

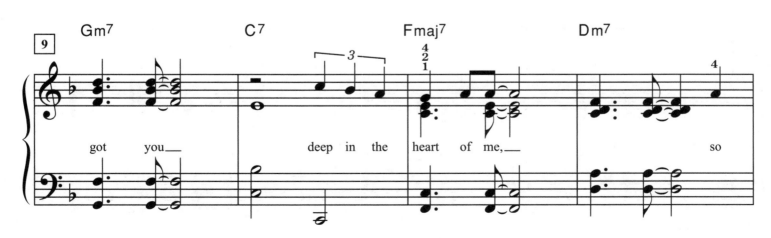

deep in my heart, you're real - ly a part of___ me.___ I've

got you___ un - der my skin. I

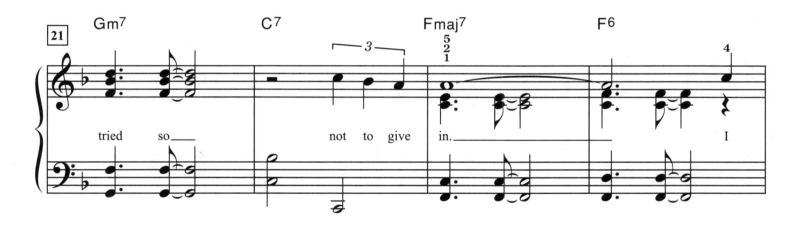

tried so___ not to give in.___ I

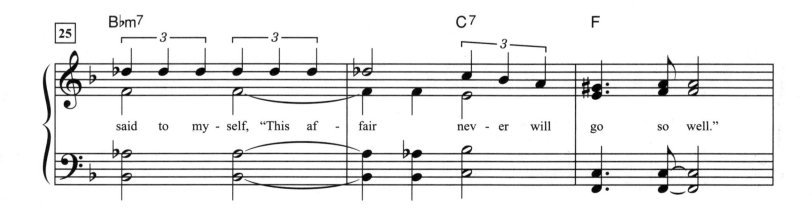

said to my - self, "This af - fair nev - er will go so well."

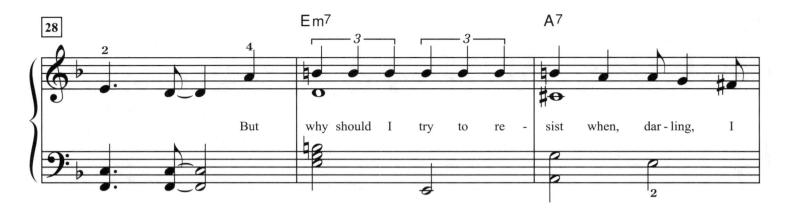

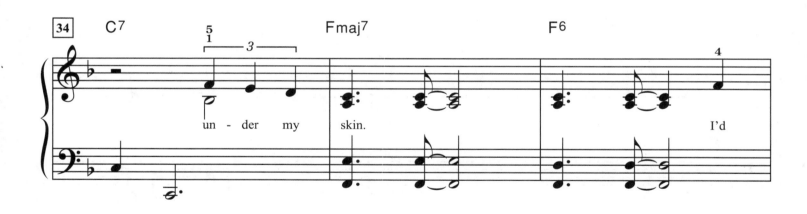

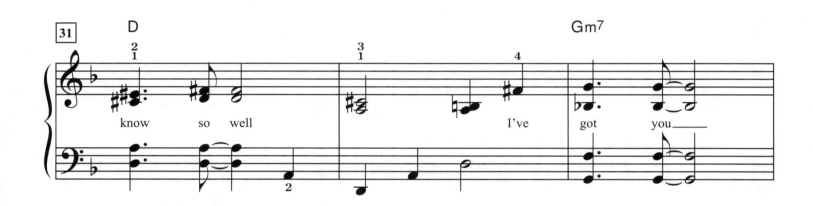

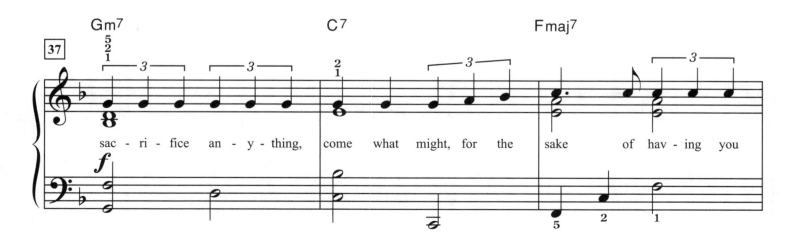

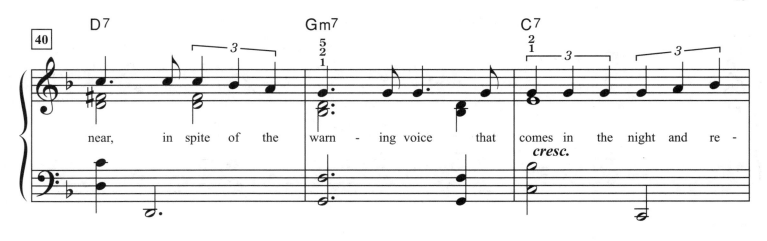

near, in spite of the warn - ing voice that comes in the night and re - *cresc.*

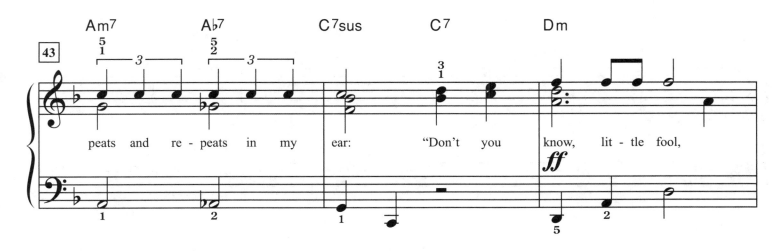

peats and re - peats in my ear: "Don't you know, lit - tle fool, *ff*

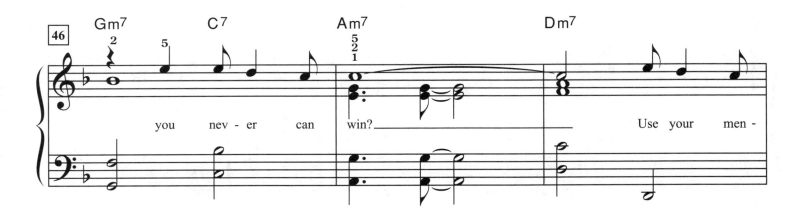

you nev - er can win?_____ Use your men -

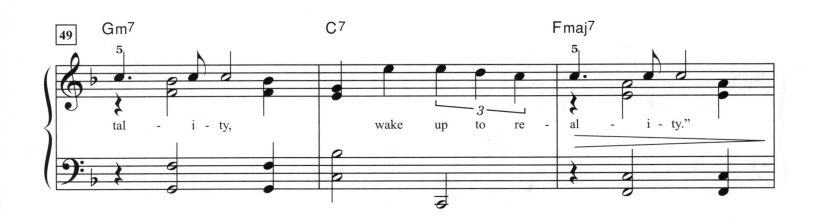

tal - i - ty, wake up to re - al - i - ty."

THE LADY IS A TRAMP

Words by Lorenz Hart
Music by Richard Rodgers
Arranged by Dan Coates

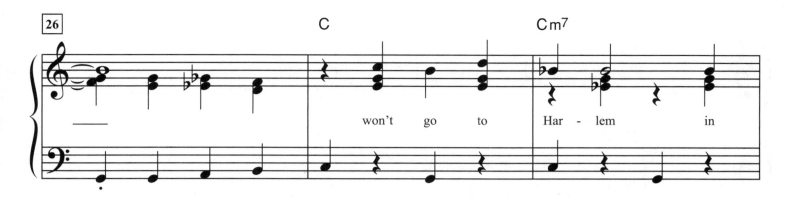

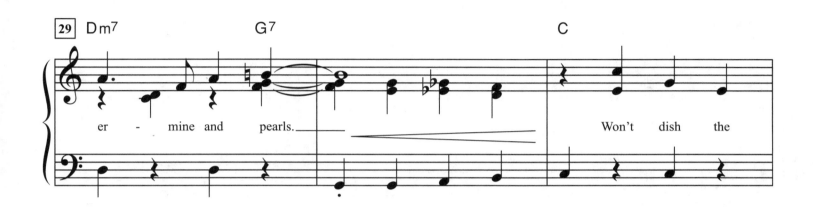

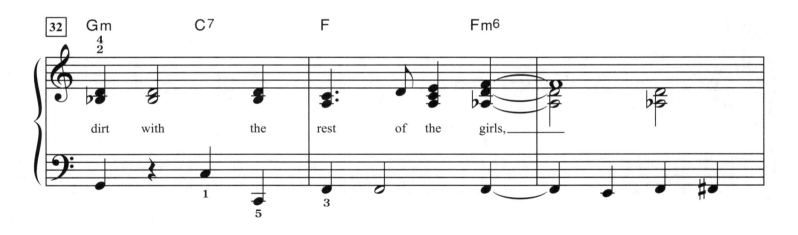

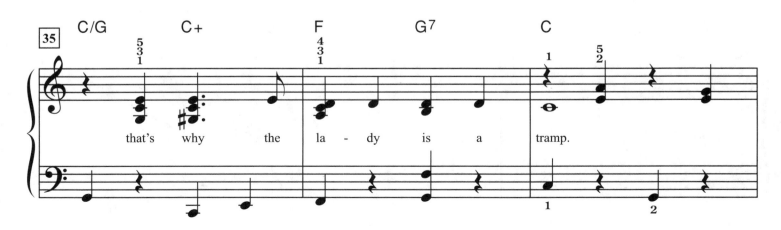

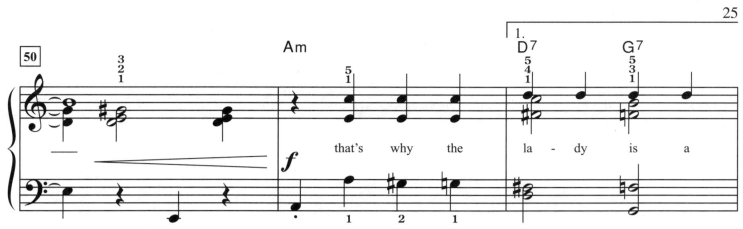

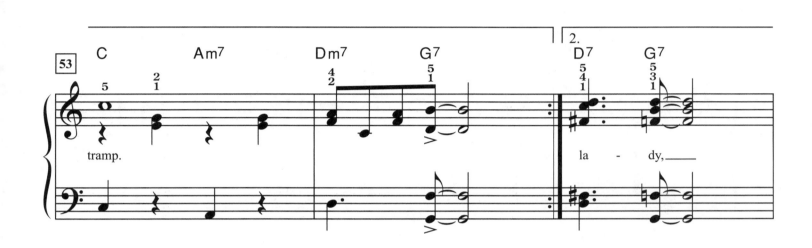

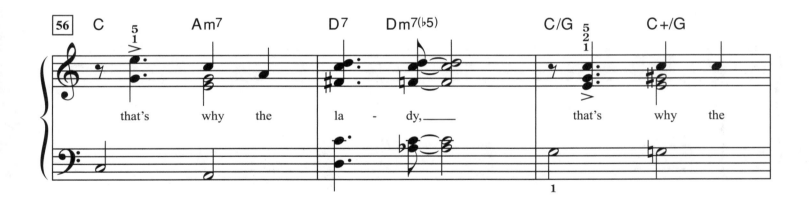

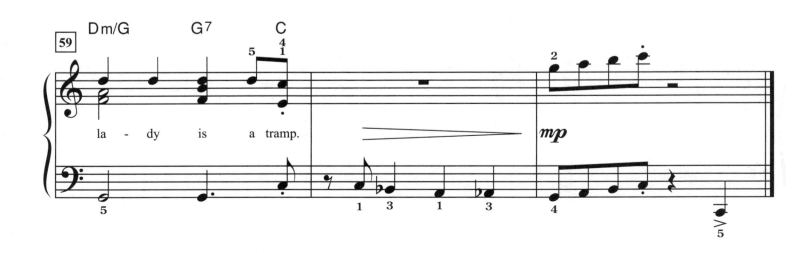

MISTY

Words by Johnny Burke
Music by Erroll Garner
Arranged by Dan Coates

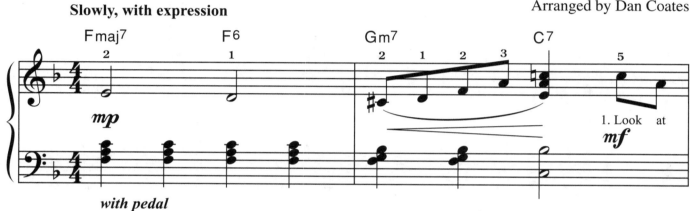

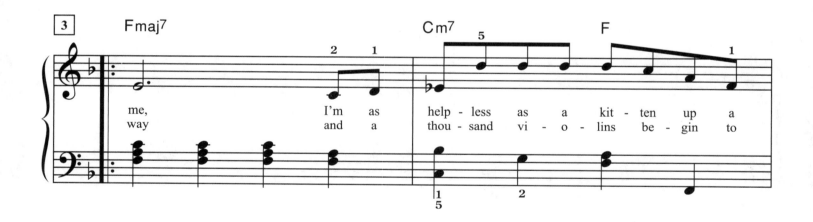

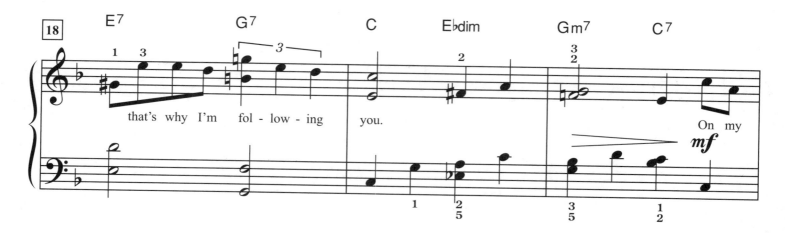

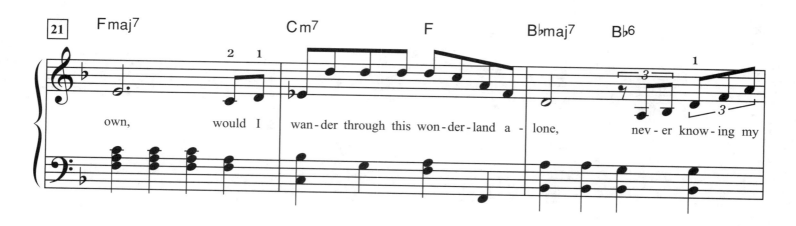

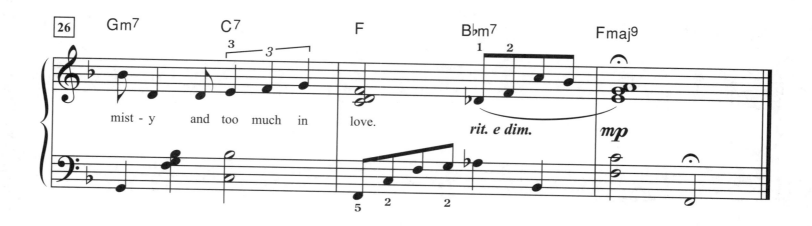

MY FUNNY VALENTINE

Words by Lorenz Hart
Music by Richard Rodgers
Arranged by Dan Coates

VOLARE

Music by Domenico Modugno
Arranged by Dan Coates

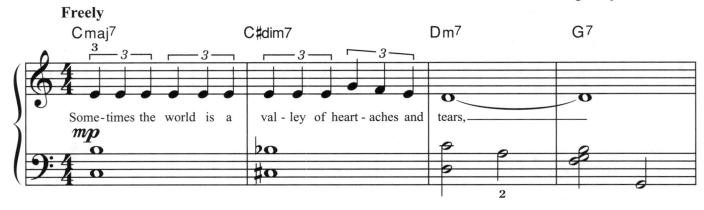

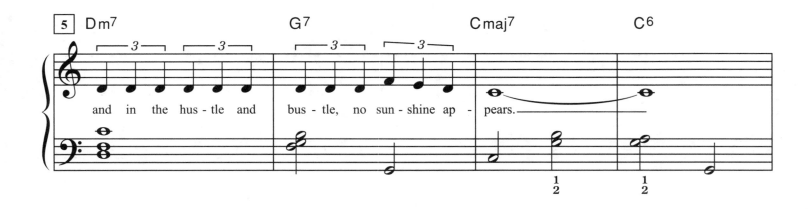

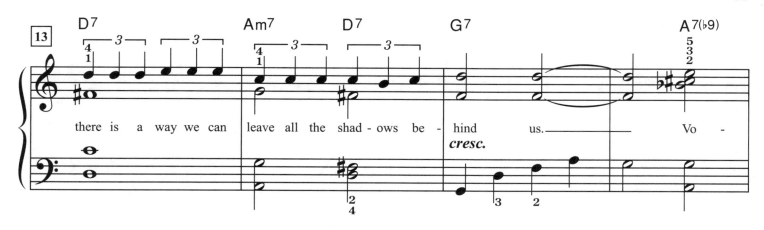

there is a way we can leave all the shad - ows be - hind us. ___ Vo -

cresc.

Moderately, with a steady beat

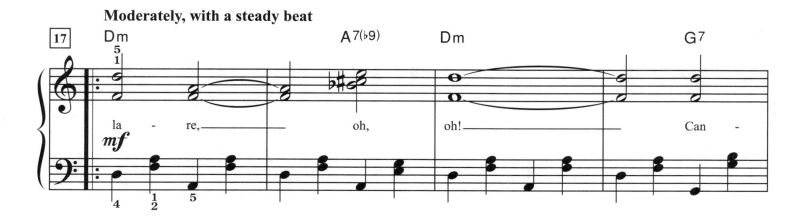

la - re, ___ oh, oh! ___ Can -

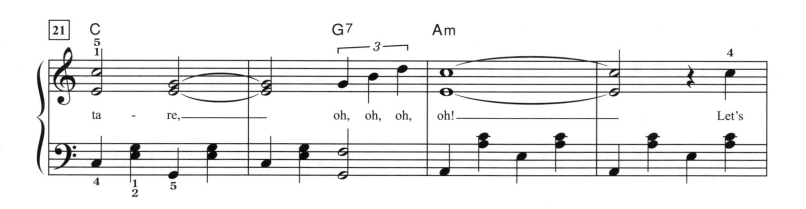

ta - re, ___ oh, oh, oh, oh! ___ Let's

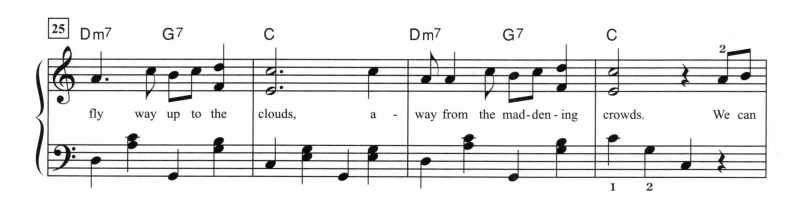

fly way up to the clouds, a - way from the mad - den - ing crowds. We can

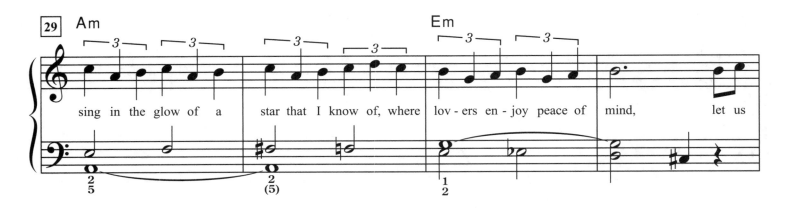

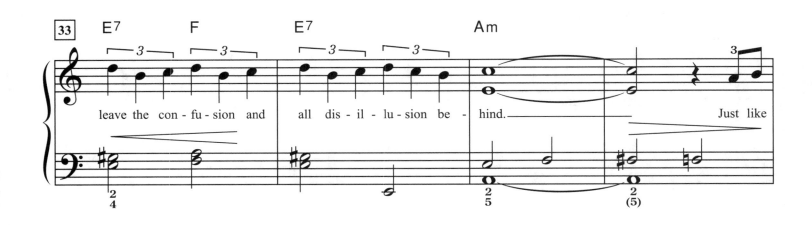

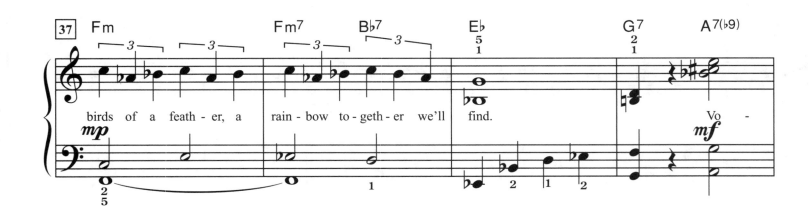

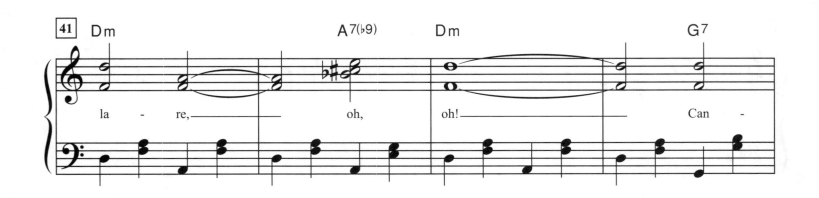

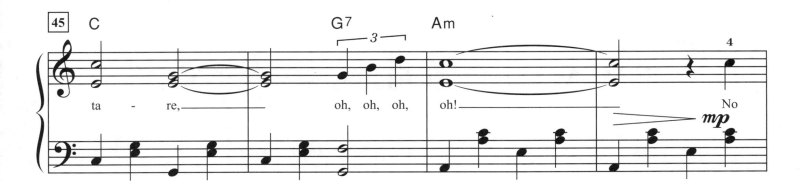

ta - re, ___ oh, oh, oh, oh! ___ No

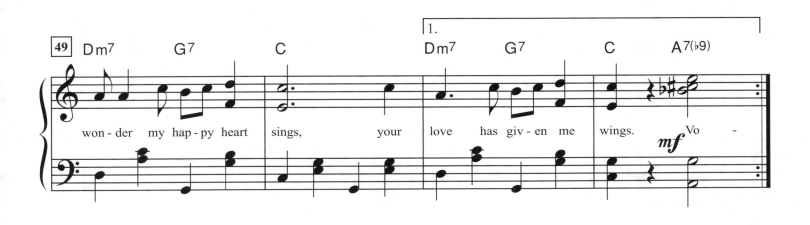

won - der my hap - py heart sings, your love has giv - en me wings. Vo -

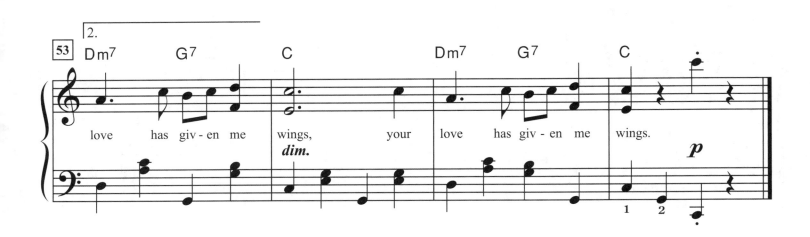

love has giv - en me wings, your love has giv - en me wings.

YOU MAKE ME FEEL SO YOUNG

Words by Mack Gordon
Music by Josef Myrow
Arranged by Dan Coates

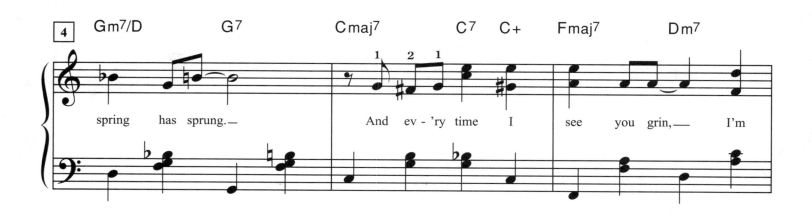

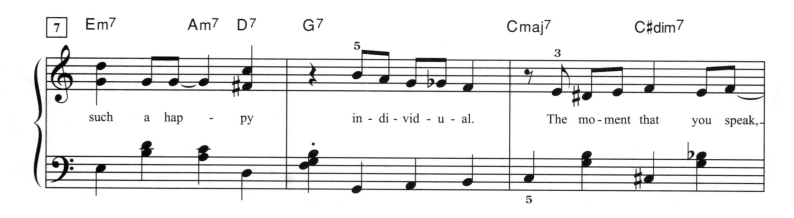

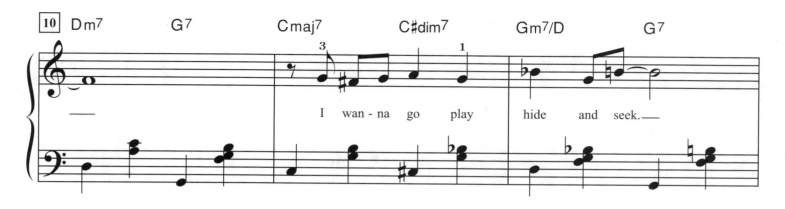

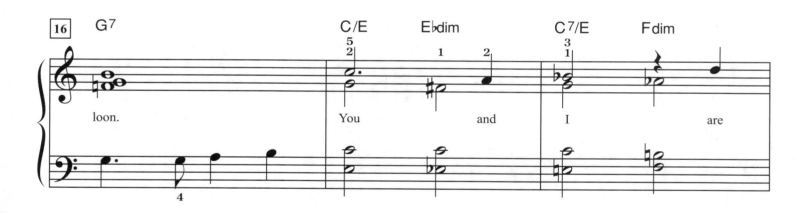

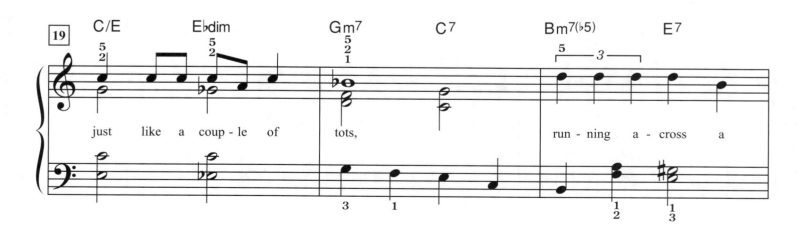

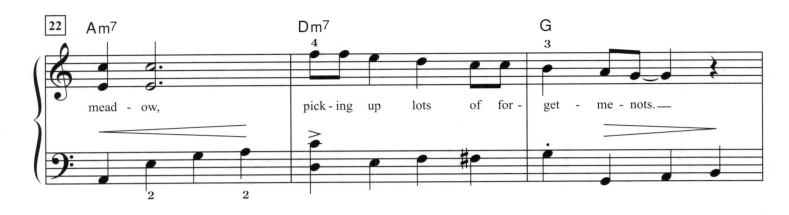

22 Am7 Dm7 G

mead - ow, pick - ing up lots of for - get - me - nots. —

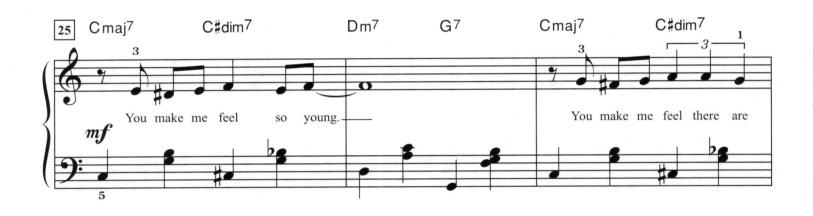

25 Cmaj7 C#dim7 Dm7 G7 Cmaj7 C#dim7

mf

You make me feel so young. — You make me feel there are

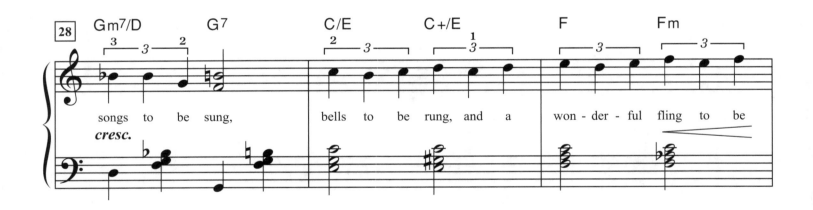

28 Gm7/D G7 C/E C+/E F Fm

songs to be sung, bells to be rung, and a won - der - ful fling to be

cresc.

31 C/E Em7 Ebm7 Dm7 G7/F Em7 Am7

flung. And e - ven when I'm old and gray,

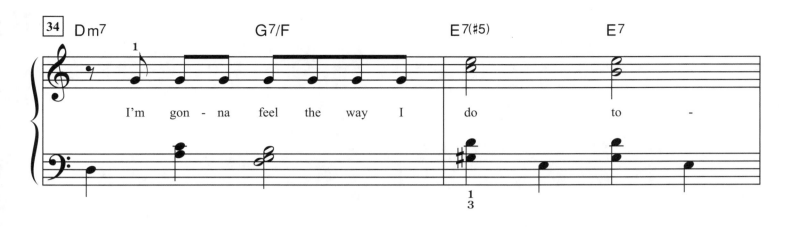

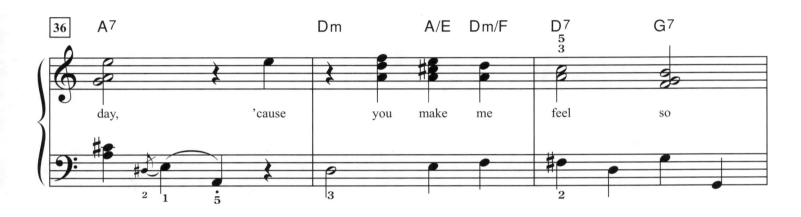

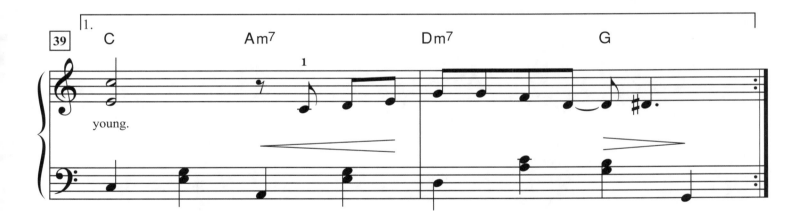